Books written and/or edited by Merle Molofsky

Jew-Hating: The Black Milk of Civilization, (edited), IPBooks, 2023

Pedro Almodóvar: A Cinema of Desire, Passion and Compulsion (coedited), IPBooks, 2019

Necessary Voices: A Collection of Short Fiction, IPBooks, 2019

Streets 1970, IPBooks, 2015

Mad, Crazy Love: Love Poems and Mad Songs, Poets Union Press, 2011

Ladder of Words, Poets Union Press, 2011

Embodied by Word Music, Poets Union Press, 2010

Correspondences, (edited), Poets Union Press, 2010

Notes for a Journey, Limbo bar& grill books, 1985

Hexagram, (edited), Poets Union Press, 1977

SH'MA, I HEAR VOICES

by Merle Heidi Molofsky

IPBOOKS.net
International Psychoanalytic Books

International Psychoanalytic Books
New York • http://www.IPBooks.net

Published by IPBooks, Queens, NY
Online at: www.IPBooks.net

Cover layout and design by Blackthorn Studio
https://blackthornstudio.com

Dedication page photo of Jonathan Molofsky and his shofar by Aideen Nunan

Interior layout and design by Noel S. Morado
https://www.linkedin.com/in/noel-morado-76469129/

ISBN: 978-1-956864-74-8

Dedication

The Creative Spirit

"Mitákuye-Oyás'in"
"All My Relations — We Are All Related"
– Lakota saying, prayer of harmony

I and Thou
– Martin Buber

Amplifying the Voices of Humanity

Sh'ma, I Hear Voices

IN GRATITUDE

Thank you to my family, friends, mentors, teachers, who appreciated and responded to my vision.

Thank you, my beloved husband, Les Von Losberg, who has shared our life together with love, depth, and delight, and who has been a precious companion and creative partner. We met as poets, became sweethearts, and continue to live together as poets and sweethearts.

Thank you, dear parents, Sima Lee Edelstein Molofsky and Samuel Molofsky, of blessed memory, who brought me into the world with a poet's soul, and who nurtured my creativity.

Thank you, my dear brother, Jonathan Molofsky, my lifelong companion, who so often shares my vision, and who cherishes our common cultural knowledge.

Thank you, dear Uncle Fred Edelstein of blessed memory, who patiently kept me on our family path, true to our family vision, when I was a teenager easily influenced by other ways of looking at the world.

Thank you, my beloved children, Rebecca, Dominic, and Sarah Francesca, who have brought me great joy, and taught me the true meaning of love and life.

Thank you, my beloved grandchildren, Anthony Joseph, Joseph Michael, Elijah, Hailey, Kane, Nick, and my beloved great-grandchildren, Sovay Lena and Esme June, who continue our family vision and traditions.

Thank you, the generations of ancestors who lived and loved, and whose endurance created the possibilities of the future for their descendants.

Thank you, those who have joined my family and contributed new vision and traditions, my sister-in-law Aideen, my son-in-law Anthony Sr., my son's companion Erica, my granddaughter-in-law Arielle, my granddaughter-in-law Grace, my granddaughter's companion Martin.

Thank you, Helen Goldberg, my psychoanalyst, who encouraged me to embark on my psychoanalytic education when I became fascinated with psychoanalytic process during our work together.

Thank you, Art Robbins of blessed memory, my mentor and teacher, who helped shape my psychoanalytic vision, and created opportunities for me to grow and to share my knowledge.

Thank you, Gerald Gargiulo, dear friend, colleague, teacher, mentor, fellow poet, who has had faith in me since we met when he taught a class in which I enrolled at our psychoanalytic institute, gave me career opportunity, and contributed to my continuing evolution as a psychoanalyst.

Thank you, Michael Eigen, whose creative psychoanalytic vision inspired me to stay true to my vision, and who is a true teacher.

Thank you, Leila Lerner of blessed memory, and Robert Mollinger, my supervisors during my psychoanalytic education at our institute, for your wisdom and patience and encouragement.

Thank you, Moses Wexler, my supervisor for an internship early in my practice, who encouraged my vision.

Thank you, cherished friends Dana Zwanziger, Sue Bloland, Lucille Spira, Douglas Maxwell, Lee Jenkins, Michael Connolly, who shared such varied experiences and interests with me.

Thank you, Robert Jokel, gifted healer, and Lawrence LeShan of blessed memory, who individually and together encouraged me to value my poetry, to keep writing my poetry, and to strive to publish my poetry. Thank you for believing in me.

Thank you, Richard Reichbart, for writing your lovely, appreciative Introduction to these poems.

Thank you, Kathy Kovacic, for your lovely cover illustration.

Thank you, Arnold Richards and Arlene Kramer Richards, who have been so supportive in publishing my fiction, poetry, and psychoanalytic writings, and to Tamar Schwartz and Larry Schwartz, and Noel Morado, who are such an important part of International Psychoanalytic Books.

ACKNOWLEDGMENTS: PREVIOUSLY PUBLISHED POEMS

Clarity

In *Bitterroot*, Vol. XVIII, No. 72, Summer 1980

Elegy

In *Hexagram*, Poets Union Press, 1977

Fair Game

In *Hexagram*, Poets Union Press, 1977

Female

In B*rooklyn Ferry: 10 New York Poets*, Brooklyn Ferry
Poets Collaborative, 1975

For Lee

In *Pig Iron*, No, 7, May 1980

For Susan

In Chapter 4, "Monumental losses, monumental gifts: analysand
and analyst mourn the death of an analyst", chapter co-written with

Vanessa Hannah Bright, poem written by Merle Molofsky, *What Happens When the Analyst Dies*, edited by Claudia Heilbrum, Routledge, London and New York, 2020, pp. 61–78.

Lost Voices

In *Psychological Perspectives*, Vol. 63, No. 2, September 2020

Office on Second Street

In *Bitterroot*, Volume XX, No. 80/81, Winter 1982/Spring 1983

Transgressors

In *The Psychoanalytic Review*, Vol.100, Issue 5, 2013, p. 767

Contents

CONTENTS

INTRODUCTION

by Richard Reichbart

It is an honor to write this introduction to a book of collected poems by Merle Molofsky, and a responsibility, as if I am a factotum standing at the threshold of a house, who sweeps his arm along in a bowing gesture of greeting and says "Enter, please." I could add, appropriately: "Enter at your own risk!".

For these are strong and haunting poems many of which – in their cadences and words – go to the very heart of things, and thus they will echo in your mind long after you have read them. And, in addition, they speak not just of joy but of darkness and conflict and the inexorable passage of time and yes, death.

Whereas today much of poetry can sound like warmed-over prose sometimes arranged in supposedly artistic patterns on the page to adopt the *appearance* of poetry, Merle's poetry is devoted to sounds to stir you with their unexpected rhythms, their often taut and sudden rhymes, and meanings that bring you up short – the way real poetry does.

Here is an early and so very simple example, from "Part One: Hearing Voices", that echoed for me long after reading because it spoke so much to the passage of time that we all experience:

1

NOW
It took a long time to grow this old,
to tell a story I've never told
and if the story prove false or true
grass still grows green and the sky's still blue.
I didn't change the world.

In fact, although Merle's poetry is sometimes obscure, it invariably is so visceral in its words that it seems to make your body respond. Here are two examples that also stayed with me long after reading:

from *LOST VOICES*
All the sages say, "Inquire within," and I howl in protest,
"I'll inquire without! I'm doing without!, It's your fault." I shout.
"You've transgressed! I've regressed! I'm oppressed! I'm obsessed!"
What's this about?

And from a remarkable poem that depicts a child's experience at the water's edge who wants the adult to take photographs and the adult's internal reactions:

Are those ducks?
Can you eat ducks?
Take a picture of you eating ducks,

the mallard-green headfeathers
making an old-fashioned
photograph of my grandmother's second-best dress.
Can I eat my grandmother, my grandmother's second-best
velvet?

Be prepared to be unsettled at times by Merle's poetry, which often focuses on the skin that marks the boundary that separates each of us and is replete with images of disintegration and loss. Here is an example from a poem called "Logic and I: In Duet":

A skull in a baby bonnet
bobs at the side of the boat.
Logic and I have agreed'
the thing wouldn't float
and now it has surfaced.

An image which to this day, as happens often with her poems, I cannot shake.

In addition, Merle is a student of poetry. One of her poems, "A Theory of Influence" pays homage by employing word references, beginning with literary critic Harold Bloom, who wrote a book titled *The Anxiety of Influence: A Theory of Poetry;* W. B. Yeats, T.S. Elliot, Wordsworth, Shelley, Garcia Lorca, Peter, Paul and Mary, James Weldon Johnson, Louis Armstrong, Leonard Cohen, and many others; and cultural references, such as to Ecclesiastes and a Jain greeting.

Of course, in addition to being a poet, Merle is a psychoanalyst, and her poems that engage so successfully on the unconscious level remind us not just of life in general, but of the psychoanalytic endeavor between analyst and patient. In effect, her poetry reflects what another famous psychoanalyst, Thomas Ogden, himself a poet, has written about poetry in the way we speak and listen in life and in psychoanalysis, "A Question of Voice in Poetry and Psychoanalysis" (1998) Psychoanaltyic Quarterly, 67(3), 426–488. Says Ogden of poets: "Perhaps if we listen to the ways they go about creating life in language and bringing language to life, we might further develop our own ways of listening and finding words to describe how a person in the analytic setting goes about bringing him/herself into being through language in the process of participating in the analytic dialogue" (p. 428).

And so, whether just for the sheer love of poetry or for a recognition of how we can receive a work that speaks so effectively and in such unconscious ways to what we as analysts grapple with on a daily basis, I wave to you to come inside this book. I hope I have succeeded in intriguing you, so that you do enter.

It is well worth the visit.

PART ONE: HEARING VOICES

The Ocean's Gift

The ocean surged to shore to tell me,
"I traveled the world, I wanted to find you,
to lay before you, at your feet,
my finest filaments of white lace."

Now

It took a long time to grow this old,
to tell a story I've never told,
and if the story prove false or true,
grass still grows green and the sky's still blue.

I didn't change the world.

Inspiration

I couldn't breathe.
Yet took a breath.
Your eyes overflowed and filled my lungs
with an infinite possibility
of being.

You smiled into every pore of my skin,
my skin gasped with delight,
and the world flowed through
at last.

When I catch my breath,
are you running?
Do I taste you?

The sky laughed,
the mountains danced,
I played my flute,
your shape emerged,
cascading notes of you,
rising,
a cloud.

I played the song of the rain
and you sang the words
inside the shape of my mouth
while the flute
breathed within its own lilting life,
and I heard you say,
"breathe as I breathe,
O living earth, O clay."

Lost Voices

Lost voices howl in every storm, every gale, every wind,
and whisper in every breeze. I hear them all.

Lost voices find a home in my lungs, and teach me how to breathe.

Lost voices are howling, screaming, "Don't seethe,
scream! Scream with me!" I stand on the edge, afraid to fall,
afraid of the guilt, of the unknown sin.

All the sages say, "Inquire within", and I howl in protest,
"I'll inquire without! I'm doing without! It's your fault!" I shout.
"You've transgressed! I've regressed! I'm oppressed! I'm
obsessed!"

What's all this about?

Now that I'm breathing, my lungs spread their wings,
I'm flying, I'm singing, I'm looping the loop,
I'm loopy, I'm twirling, I'm nobody's groupie,
I'm letting it all out in one savage whoop.

And Walt Whitman chases me to the roofs of the world,
sounding his barbaric yawp – that yawp belongs to me,
and thee, and us. Walt Whitman says, "Celebrate,"
Catallus says, "Love and hate,"
Howlin' Wolf keeps howling, howling for his darling,
woo woo woo woo woo.

Back at the ranch, at the lost and found,
what goes around keeps going around,
for what was lost must now be found,
and I'd be rhyming crowned and clowned
to find that awesome rhyming sound
before that voice is drowned drowned drowned
in silence.

In the silence I'm still breathing.

Drum of heart and crawling whispers,
the beat goes on and the song will start,
matins, serenades, and vespers,
Leonard Cohen's bells that still can ring,
ring out loud for everything!

In the silence I'm still here....

Where are you? Without? I invite you in....

One Moment in Autumn

Yearning to embrace the blaze of autumn,
to hold each nuance of flame,
each transforming leaf,
each vine and branch and tree,
until all is, indelibly,
absolutely, brilliantly,
part of me.

Autumn, will you open your radiant
heart of fire,
your phoenix wings,
and take me in your arms?

And if in bleak December I should crave
the warmth of sunlight smiling in your eyes,
if I should yearn for all that once you gave,
your pulsing touch, your wordless sighs,

I'll learn to cherish silence, endless snow,
icy blasts of winds that cry your name
in memory of that ragged afterglow
that seemed to transmute clouds to story,
weaving spells, a promise: night must fall
and crash, and fragment, giving form to dawn.

Cryptic Message

Cryptic message: do not translate until instructed to do so.

Do not decode without faith.

Leaves falling, drifting past the tree of life.

Krishna playing the flute, melody breath floating

the fallen leaf

back to life.

Poem Without Pain

I should try to explain:
A morning mist,
a cloud-kissed sky,
a foghorn weeping in the rain.
Words that flow, and glow
and sigh,
cascading to become a stream.

And if by chance the trees are singing,
do we hear nigunim?
If merrily, merrily, bells are ringing
is it true life's but a dream?

If we hear birds,
do we hear klezmer?
Is their song klezmer rising?
If we hear klezmer, do we dance?
Musicians, poets, mesmerizing
with their soul-embracing chants.
O World, O riverrun of words,
O harpist's tumbling minor thirds,
bei mir bist du schoen.

Streetscape

Industrial sunset; arab
Edge of moon. Night
Song of horn and vibes:
Bright sword latent
In a swath of silks;
Smiling Salome,
Violence veiled.
Serpentine outline,
Romance of merchant
Neon: aqua, orange,
Pink: street
Counterpoint
To starlight
Startled and white
Above our doubt,
Beyond our eyes.

Our eyes.
        Our eyes
Have chanted brick
And stone a mute
And hollow grey.
Our eyes have oxidized
In Brooklyn rains all
Reds and greens of roofs, of doors,
Crying chromium colors
Into dust. As if the rain
Were dry as time, as dry as
Flame.

The metaphor: street space
Franklin/Fulton
Crux of place,
Symbol for
Texture of time.
Shabazz Steak n Take
Bensonburgers
Moving down a langorous line
Of names that mean
To be dream.

The Scarlett Lounge, the El-Sudan,
The street where transient
Children ran;
Dreamdust of
Cellophane
In evening
Rain, in
Vain.

The metaphor: take
Me for a ride.
I got nothing
To hide.

The image: woman
At a crossroads,
Squatting, like a
Toad, thumbing
Her way. She
Has something
To say.
She seems
To be alone.
She is not lame.
No matter where the wind has blown

The point of view remains
The same.
She sets a scene:
Crossroads, at the crossroads,
Looking for a free ride.

Take a chance: analyze
The motion toward meaning.
To all the questions the
Only question left
To ask:
Can you
Get me
Here.
Looking
For Now.
Just looking,
For now.

Take a taxi: dime
A dance. Hanging
In there till time
Is called. Can't
Fake it, can't break it,
Can't take it,

Can't take it nowhere,
No how. No way.

The point of view must remain
The same. And if she must ride,
She must ride pain.
Revelation on the road:
Now that she is convinced
She is here, she doesn't want to be.

Franklin Avenue/arrow
Creating time's duration,
Franklin Avenue bus
Creating time's sensation:
Intersection of changes.
Experimental eyes from
The other side of between;
Instant replay. A bleeding
Street of consciousness
Always the color of rain.
Women wobble, like children,
With the lurch, whoring
For the exact change,
The same river twice.

This is not she who has been here.
The smell of wet and gasoline
As focal as once.

Unseen

Seeing, like imaginary interstices
Of moment and point, between
Being and it, a substance
At once and gone.

Remembered

Image: woman, metaphor.
"Christ, what are patterns
For...."

She rides pain to get to here
Without necessity of medium.
Should one decipher the message:
Tedium.
The obligation exists
To communicate
Of course
Engramatically.

Symbol synthesis:
You and I
Echoes of narcissus.

Quick! There, in the blank and angry
Window, before it is gone!
See
The isolated frame:
Time, personified, catching its breath;
The shadow 'neath the cowl.
A clear white starshine neon light: Death
Shows his face. Our eyes have seen
Bone within the arching nothing spanning
Brick on brick; spirit eye
of houses blind to the rot of wait.
It is not time that change demands.

If, while posing for some standard scene
Of where and who and when,
I am the battleground,
Then
All gathered blood of wars
and warriors,

like rain, like awe,
will stain me, color me
Living.

When noticing a miracle,
Some gesture is always
Appropriate.
Within a moving space
Is closet drama,
Feeling in drag.

I have always been somewhere
Else, and someone else
Is masquerading as me.

When you look from my eyes
What do you see?
Can we, some day
Compare? I dare,
And you agree.

Verify experience, computer soul
Become binary possibility.

Words, like the jagged ruins of interval,
Clog the lubricated rhythms
Of the all-star god machine.
I Ching casts its patterns
Everywhere the mind goes:
There will be evil
No blame.

Industrial sunset; arab
Edge of moon. You,
Good friend, do you
Get the picture?
I have been where
It all happens,
And hadn't the heart to send a postcard.

Wish I were here....

Telling Tales

Chances are
in the way the story works out.
The ways in which the fine lines
intersect,
the moment touching
act.

All those congruent
places I could have been,
and all the still life
memories
after the fact.

This minor claim to being the story teller:
it's a lie.

It's more like playing games.

But if I should ask, just once,
to surrender,
could I ever
anticipate, again.

It seems it would be too obvious to bear,
this world and all its true life stories.

And if there are even other ways
of truly being,
they do not lead homeward,
or I am lost.

The Road to Damascus

Conversion:
In a former life I had been a miner,
burrowed naked, worm-like, in the mountain's flesh,
learned to read the leer of metal in unresponding rock,
learned to love the flicker of ore awakening in torchlight,
lived intimately with darkness.

On a day like all days, under an unseen brilliant sun,
I was crawling through night-space, enfolded in green hills,
and felt my mind change.

Just before the air gave out completely
the inner world exploded,
and just before I died
the labyrinth I knew so well
revealed itself a hell
of contradictions,
dead ends, secret doorways
opening on impossible perspectives,
false vistas, heretic geometries.

In another life there had been too many surfaces,

a thousand and one textures in relation to light,

and he that was I grew weary,

grew weary of wood, of honey, amber, the skin of slaves,

the limbs of young girls, of fruit ripe and unripe,

of moonlight on water, nacreous dawns

joining land and sea,

the many golds and silvers gleaming from earthy caverns,

from firmament,

yes, and round the necks of courtesans....

O he that was I grew weary of the necks,

the arms, the bellies, the flanks

of courtesans and young boys, weary of all things embraced

and embracing, of corners and crevices, the touchable,

the reachable,

the world yearned for, the distant....

Later I crouched over a basin, retching.

I did not like my sounds, my stenches,

nor did I like the unrelenting walls,

the dour floors, the ceaseless confinement of a room.

I was going to have cancer within the moment,
I could feel it circling, closing in,
and all because I had crouched over a basin,
retching, in a whiteness without windows.
Doctors readied their tools of trade.

If ever I return to Paradise, I swear I will stop mistreating my slaves.
Have I told you of the olives of my native land,
black olives oozing oil,
a miracle of texture, of lucence, of fragrance, a real delight....

On Mount Olympus

Cutting his space into
dark corners, cleaving
distances among his worlds,
only his shoulders
betray one taut
fraility: he refuses
to fight the weather
on human terms.

With no where to go
and knowing it,
he found a place to
be. Here among old
men and clattering
spoons, he chose to
become himself again,
to become a god
and know it, unafraid
of other places where he
was only man.

We create moments to
be left untouched; we
memorize impressions
with deliberate distaste
for truth. This is
time shaped for
our later years; without
each other we have
ourselves. I choose
your shoulders to remember you:
on human terms I play with gods.

Time Was When

We were living in
essential time; a
measure of feeling
between you and
me. You
of course had all
the answers, while
I, of course, still
doubted. How does
one ask
a question? There were
spaces left
in spite of the risks:
we postulated maybe
to the facts –
a criminal compliance in
need. Theoretically
we were free, and
you took account
of me, often.

Transgressors

Transgressors never really mean it:
You insist, I never transgressed beyond
the boundaries of good taste….
Yet there are other borders
to a self: we are more
than style. You took
my time and I was satisfied
with yours.
There's no defense
against the light,
and we are phototropic
together.
It is never the places you explore,
but the places you ignore,
that violate.

When you returned myself to me
I was angry, and didn't know
how to thank you.
And never having had you,
I was the sole possessor of a gift,
while you were left with my

thanks a lot.
I hope you didn't mind,
for there is nothing left to give
except these words,
and they can be had by anyone
who desires words.

Solo Duet

You who have shot the moon,
dragged your hair along the face
of the wind,
you who have filled a world
with your children,
you venture no further
than your doorway,
line your windowsills
with shards,
disturb the surfaces of things,
interfere with the view,
retreat from the horizon to home.

You have grown fuller than the sun,
you fill the sky.

I remember when you shone within me
like a secret in the night,
a hidden spice in the heart,
and I was heavy with you
as if I were earth,
the two banks of a river,
as if you were the hive,
and I the fallen tree.

There is a Raging

There is a raging in the land –

Poets smash their harps;
there comes forth a music
mad as stone.

The body rips loose from the beating heart,
the puppet twists from the animate hand.

In a white frenzy of city-carved space,
the subtle embalming begins.
We laminate the zoo and gild the garden.

A dancer moves alone
past a masquerade of death,
an insect skimming the surface of the waters,
inebriate among shadows.

A painter shoots paint pointblank
at a two-dimensional skin,
disemboweling form within.

Welcome to the autopsy, welcome to the feast.
There's no distinguishing mannerist from beast
in a time of crisis.

Timing Sonnet

The door is locked. It must be half-past six.
We've come too late. I'd planned to buy new shoes,
a hat, a string of pearls. This really ticks
me off. Whose fault is it? I don't care whose,
although it's clearly yours. You always seem
to dawdle when we have no time to spare.
Don't start in now with "life is but a dream",
or "we are merely players". I don't care
to talk philosophy or hear your line
about what we should value most. I need
to spend my money. Your words sound fine,
but they don't soothe as you believe. The harm
is done. No sale. Illusion has such charm.

Sky Dreaming

The pug-snarl of a Tibetan demon
unfurls from a cloud clot,
leers across the sky,
and then d—i—s—s—o—l—v—e—s.
An angry eye discovers
charging pigs, wolf-faced cherubs,
animal herds stampeding toward
their northern burial ground.
Distant bodies, arranged like tomato wedges
scattered over the penthouse roof
of the Pickwick Arms,
make demands of the sky.

The sky remains blue, calm,
a young mother with sheltering shoulders,
with cloud breasts in a nearly cloudless sky,
absorbing the city as if it were a hungry lover.

What Is This and When Is Now

This is my room. My bed,
my window, my knee,
my eyebrow, my ski
pajamas, my closet,
my night, my dark,
my witch, my nightmare,
my terror, my feet,
my floor, my I can't run,
my I can't scream,
my blanket, my head,
my burrow, my shaking,
my sleep, my sleep,
sleep. This is my name.

World. This is a world.
Name the world and all
its parts. Name
the animals. Gain dominion.
Lose and gain a world.
Gain a world and lose
a soul.

The fundamental problem,
it seems to me now,
is that no one has yet told me
my secret name.

There is safety in numbers.
Count down. Start from
infinity and work backwards.
Wake me when you get to
number one – look out
for it.

This is you. This is
your real name. This is
your room, your bed, your window,
your knee, your eyebrow.
This doesn't count.
Count me out.
You, me, you, me, you, me,
our skin between us,
like a name
we cannot remember.

Child at the Water's Edge

He reads the signs
but not the meanings,
like sunlight and water
move together on wood
like colors of fish are their markings
and the patterns of their feedings
in the skin of waters
also markings,
also signs.

> Take a picture of the ducks –
> What's that? Is that
> a turtle?
> Take a picture of the turtle.

What do the ducks mean
when they search, and
eat, and quarrel over
food?

Are those ducks?
Can you eat ducks?
Take a picture of you eating ducks,

the mallard-green headfeathers
making an old-fashioned
photograph of my grandmother's second-best dress.
Can I eat my grandmother, my grandmother's second-best
velvet?

Take a picture of the goldfish:
I'm the one who discovered it.
Can I take a picture?

Can I take a picture
of my words for goldfish,
turtles, ducks; my words
for appetite?

The child who asks such questions
lives within a camera, soon after she is born.
Lives inside her language, holds back being
with questions.

Wood moves with water,
with sunlight, moves
with meaning.

The question that answers itself moves against
meaning, and then is still.

When the voice sings
the answers listen.

      Look at all the colors,
      Black…white,
      Black and white.
      Gold…white,
      White and gold.

White is paler
under water,
under green
and sunlight
flexing,
clotting into diamonds.

Mommy, look.
Look at.
A bee's drownding.

Poor bees.

I hate them.

Child goes elsewhere
as cloud numbs
sunlight…water…wood
into memory.

Memory, as numb
as anything but now.
Now she reads
the signs, now
means the meaning.

Logic and I: In Duet

A skull in a baby bonnet
bobs at the side of the boat.
Logic and I have agreed
the thing wouldn't float
and now it has surfaced.
With all deliberate speed
we bash at the head
as if it were a torpedo.
It is. Logic and I
are compelled to explode.
A skull in a baby bonnet
bobs at the side of the boat.
I float downstream
as if Ophelia had never been written.
Stars in sudden profusion
admire their eyes in the water.

It must be night,
the dark hours
to which we are entitled,
by virtue of birth,
R & R at carefully timed
intervals, in which
we invent worlds
equally _____.

At this point
the skull in the bonnet
suggests "malevolent", "abhorrent",
"obscene", "grotesque". All the while
grinning. Grin your fool head off,
there are other words to fill the blanks,
I suggested. Logic and the baby
continue to drift upstream.

Seen Through the Eye

Over there
a man ogles a woman with a baby.
He likes the way she looks like soft sounds
would come forth from her when squeezed:
a mama-doll.

Woman mangles baby-doll: soft wounds.

Yonder
a daughter colors story-pictures,
a montage of boredom, mother-dry,
more and again, repeating:
"Look, here's the witch,
the wicked witch,
will carry you away."
How her mother nods her head, how she sighs,
dark hair sleek and parted,
the rose behind her ear, in her teeth, at her waist,
breasts that jiggle and bob.
It's an acrobatic act, a wonder,
that there are witches,
that the story comes true.

Over yonder
magic words are spoken,
round black beads on a golden thread.

Over there
a man ogles a woman with a baby....
He likes them broken in.

Female

Shadows in the form of
walls; handwriting
in the form of shadows.
Muted warnings in
the owl's call,
the mouse's answering silence.

Night is as predatory
as ever we are;
larger, more muscular,
less vulnerable.

I heard the black
wings of an owl
scratch upon
a copper shield her
secret:
Mother Night hides
her bush soul on the dark side
of the moon.

Before the Facts

Life changes before the facts do.

Consider – a meadow, new as morning,
a-dazzle with dew, hay-sweetened,
warm, still, and a deer,
suddenly more still.
                    Perhaps
the wind shifts, or a predator enters,
laughing, perhaps adrenalin
practices its kick against the shivering
trees beyond, or a grasshopper click,
or the shadow of a cloud – consider
middle age.

This morning you woke up dreaming
of angels, to the radio-alarm
perfection of Jessie Norman
singing Amazing Grace,
as the dee jay signed While the City Sleeps
off the air. O! the dream
persisted throughout the day,
a tatter of miracle to wrap against

the chill demands
of worldly affairs, the fact
of time grinding girl into grandmother,
grace into guilt.

This morning a boy leaps in the air
playing at conquest, playing ball,
and your back twinges at the echo
of that leap in your flesh.

You sit in the backwash
of the setting sun, and rest,
broad-lapped, close your eyes,
and pray for nothing more than this....

Point of No Return in Shades of Grey

And if there were a black swan flying north,
what then? And if the wind
had teeth, so that men
called her female, what matter?
All I know is that the day lingered too long
into the evening, and the wind
evened the score, so that the sky
was marked by her, as if by claws.
The black swan soared overhead
like a sign.

                The house was a cat,
claws tucked, hunched against the rain,
and I stood in the doorway as a token.
Between home and the road
twilight poured itself around me
like honey. When the lightning
struck and the storm broke,
I leaped halfway between
moonlight and burning.

Now all I want is springtime, bunches of lilacs
in a vase, and a window.
At the edge of the lawn, where the woods begin,
a cat is about to pounce
upon a bird about to fly.

Yes, and often I dream
I am walking.

Once Upon a Time

there was a man, new-born, and no woman.
She was somewhere else, resting.
He was new-born, almost a tree,
not looking for her. He was alone
with the earth, and his nostrils
were wide open. She felt him
coming, and her hips moved.
Her bones began to sing,
in imitation of water,
when he arrived, a man,
new-born, unable to see her.
Therefore she gathered the world
in her arms, gathered dry leaves,
clumps of grass, sod, earthworms,
and her bosom smelled like grapes,
like early autumn just before frost.

O there was a man, new-born,
smooth as a willow, and O
his eyes reflected everything,
so of course he couldn't see her
when she came running with all the sky
burning alive in her hair and the earth
always at her feet as if in worship.

She climbed a tree, became a bird,
held to the air in a rush of wings,
fell down. She was soft among the grasses.
Pebbles bit her. She didn't care.
"Nothing hurts if you can't fly."
He rooted his fingers into the soil,
howled at the sky alive and wriggling
in its own pale trap.

"The moon is caught in the trees,"
the man saw, and his lips moved
and he wondered and he grew up.
But the moon escaped, and wandered
loose in the daylight, a cow
calf-hungry, lowing, "Where are
all my children?"

The woman couldn't get free of it,
you know, she died of it.
Now all flowers
are fated to fall; it is their
own choosing. And the man is old;
trees bend over him in winter
to keep him from looking upward.
The woman is dead, dead
and there is a bird
and there is a bird flying.

Blood Test

The hook of the new moon
has caught my heart tonight;
Night is blood-colored,
   earth-scented.
Something runs apace with the wind,
Female, with nostrils open,
a mare,
perhaps.
The wind shifts; the animal,
like a river, moves on.
Night smells of iron,
and the moon, a glass shard,
is spattered with blood.

Morning.
The wheat is on fire,
the mountain brook talks in tongues,
twists mad as a man
in its grass corset.
Obsessed with the illusion of escape
the trees, crucified by birdsong,
are nailed to the day.

Here a red fox sleeps,
there the ground is wet
with rabbit blood.

We are women,
Weaving, and there is war.
A mare screams, scarlet thread
on a grey field, and we are women
Weaving. We tattoo into our skirts
whimpers of children,
and the golden bones of their hands
as they died among us.

Death is the sound of water,
a mud- and root-scented wind;
Memory is syrupy as night. O
I am caught at the point
of blood.

Grief and Celebration
for Susan Harding

GRIEF:

We looked out on a sudden wilderness—

No grass, no trees, just barren rock and clay.

Left with nothing, or even less,

We stared at a world bleached and empty, somber and grey.

We heard a thieving raven cry,

Saw jagged ragged mountains butchering the sky.

CELEBRATION:

She danced as Zohar, forever touched by light,

Radiant with ecstasy, glowing with delight.

She sang with joyous freedom, in silver tones a-shimmer,

And laughed with joyous freedom, giving all a glimmer

Of celestial spheres at play.

And so today

She lives and sings and dances in every mind and heart

Forever a deep part

Of each of us who loved her.

Remember

To celebrate her life, a radiant blazing flame, each ember

Warm and loving, giving, caring

Full of joy, daring

To be free.

Zohar, you will always be

Incandescent in our memory.

September 18, 2010, In Memoriam

Freedom

"Freedom's just another word for nothing left to lose"
– Kris Kristoferson

When you run out of options
and you have no choice,
when you know you're forsaken
and you've lost your voice,
when your heart beats faster
than the storm winds blow,
and you seek a master
to tell you which way to go –

that's a head-on collision with freedom.

My mother told me stories,
my father sang me songs,
my brother shares my memories
and I sit and count the wrongs,
the trials and tribulations
all piled up in a heap,
despair and grim resentment,
dreams that slaughter sleep –

that's the basic condition of freedom.

"Tell me where shall I go,
Vo ahin zoll ich geyn,"
Home.

Doors don't have to open,
eyes don't have to smile,
just as long as I know
the eternal is worthwhile.

"Children," teacher says,
"Write a poem about freedom."
Heads bow over wooden desks,
each hand clutches a pen,
the paper lies expectant,
and then says, "When!"
Now the poems happen,
spill across the room,
crawl along the woodwork,
linger in the gloom.
The evening star is rising,
the sun's already set,
the moon is still surprising
teacher's pet.

"Teacher, I thought I aced it,
I thought you might approve.
Now it's late, you've got a date,
and I still haven't found my groove."

Poem, keep on singing,
freedom, keep on ringing.
I heard a bird crying –
I felt myself flying –

There's no one to accuse,
and there's nothing left to prove –

QED.

Searching for the Light

I. PILGRIM

I was born a pilgrim
searching for the Light,
found a world of wilderness,
wild and weird and bright.

Told my heart I had to know
what was wrong and right,
thought that all I had to do
was learn to walk upright.

II. JOURNEY

First I heard the music,
heard Harp and Voice entwine.
Then I saw the Garden,
with grass and tree and vine.

I climbed into the branches
and chose the sweetest fruit,
I rested high above the earth
and listened to a flute.

The trill of birdsong wound around
the lingering melody,
and though my heart was full of joy
I heard a threnody.

The scent of roses filled the air,
a stream splashed far below,
and sunshine turned the world to gold
as I watched the waters flow.

Next I crossed a desert,
slogging through the sand,
beaten low beneath the Light
and fearing the demand

that I must suffer, I would sin,
I would lose my way,
the threnody I heard was my regret
that Night would conquer Day.

Again I heard a water sound,
heard surging tide roll in.
I heard the crash of waves arrive,
I heard a frenzied din

of earthquake and tsunami,
and I was now at sea,
buffeted and tossed around
and wishing I were free,

wishing I were still on land,
and hoping land was stable,
and yet I found myself dragged down,
deep down, yet strangely able

to breathe in water like a fish,
to swim into a cave,
into a darkness so intense
I began to rant and rave.

I found a secret grotto,
and hid within the gloom,
and understood my mourning song
foretold a hideous doom.

I found the source of the River Styx,
I knew the tenebrous cloud.
I swam into the stygian core,
was buried, cried aloud.

III. THE CALL

Again I heard a sun-filled song
with words I took within,
the words sang, Light and Dark are one,
and each one needs its twin.

If I embrace the Darkness,
and trust my truest core,
the Light will shine forever,
forever ever more.

Yom Kippur: A Prayer Offered to A Prayer Offered

The Book of Jonah is read on Yom Kippur —
We study to understand why —

How many times we are asked, and say no,
how many times must we say no to discover yes?
When we are called to answer, the status quo
default is chaos, and the truth is anybody's guess.

A prophet on the waters is no different from a sailor
on the land. Out of our element, unable to stand
and face the demand to challenge folly, lift our hand
and reach for guidance from a Voice that spanned
the heavens and the sea, the earth and inner depths,
to reach the sad reluctant heart, the Jonah-heart
that cries out, "Lord, why me?"

Yes atones for no.
If I am called, must I go?

A Theory of Influence

an inevitable misprision, either accidental or deliberate, or neither,
of *The Anxiety of Influence: A Theory of Poetry,* by Harold Bloom

I. THE GIFT

We see Nothing
because we can see.

Shadows of Nothing
ripple through Light.
Starbursts of Something
penetrate Night.

Remember the First Time
before you were born.
Remember the End Time –
Destruction! then morn.

II. RECEIVING THE GIFT

In order to understand the language of the birds
we lick honey off the page,
discover Aleph,
then Beit, in the beginning,
a world within a Book
was the Word,
within the Book a Garden,
and the Word was with....
and the Word was....

Within the Garden a fountain,
where water flowed like music,
where music flowed like words,
where words flowed language,
the language of the birds,
wild with poetry.

III. SHARING THE GIFT

Whoever is listening,
      co-create.
Word-music lives in I-Thou.
Guide for the perplexed:
      Be here now – and how –

IV. CLINAMEN

Atoms have their own learning curve,
celebrating at random,
with reckless joy and verve.
Atoms atomopomorphize
mathematics and humankind,
a tyranny of unpredictability
evolving in order to find
no fixity, kaleidoscope
of time and space,
a zero-sum no winners or losers
relay race.

Poets, as the atoms swerve,
feel along your every nerve
collision with who's sung before,
singing from a common core.

If you must sing, then you must serve.
Find the ancestors you want to deserve.

V. TESSERA

"Lift every voice and sing"
mosaic of every song once sung,
now singing, ringing,
echo of the future
welcoming each note
home again.

If every word takes its
      once and future
      ever-lasting
      always
      now

place in the great mandala,
Who spins the wheel of fortune?
whose number always is coming up?
I've been singing the same song, daddy,
since Hector was a pup.

VI. KENOSIS

I accept and refuse –
I will sacrifice only for fulfillment.
If nothing can be sole or whole
if it hasn't been torn or rent,
then will I for a moment
eviscerate all words within,

      repent, repent,

      assent, assent,

until all my ancestors relent.

Free verse? What could be worse?
What could be worse is the curse
of longing. Imitation is the hearse
in which imagination lies.

Sing, O Muse, a terse eulogy
ripe with tripe, in which we immerse
the caged bird. Shape-shifting bird,
become a fish. I'll throw a coin
and make a wish. Feed the multitudes.
Fish become Word.

VII. DAEMONIZATION

Define Identification:
    I admire you.
    I want to be like you.
I want to curl myself around your beauty
until your beauty is mine.

Define Beauty:
    The object of desire.
    The Path to the Path.
    The primal element, Fire,
    the procreative soul of Wrath.
    Ahimsa.
    Shanti.

The cooling bath
of Word made Flesh
where Flesh can mesh
with Word. Absurd.
And true.
The bird is you.

O.
Now I know.
At least for now.
I want my words,
my truth, my ancient memories,
my song
to be exactly what I am.
To do as you have done.
There's nothing new under the sun
except me.

VIII. ASKESIS

The pond is empty.
Basho's frog longs for water.
Dry summer. No splash.

Froggie went a-courting and he sings the blues,
A-hum, a-hum.
You don't miss your water 'til your well runs dry.
If mermaids sing, and not to me,
if Suzanne takes you down, and fills your cup,
beaded bubbles winking at the brim,
and purple-stained your greedy mouth,
the gold that glitters may be sand,
or sunrise, sundown, heavenly alchemy,
after long silence, let there be speech
that transcends understanding.

My mind cannot be
empty. No. I gasp for breath
and lose track of time.

IX. APOPHRADES

*A pamphlet, no matter how good, is never read more than once, but a
song is learned by heart and repeated over and over.* — Joe Hill

Alfred Hayes wrote the words, and Earl Robinson the music,
together they taught us Joe Hill never died.

I dreamed I heard an angelic choir – Yeats and Leonard Cohen,
Willie the Shake and that great vaudeville team Sheets and Kelly.
I couldn't resist. I'll name them now, Keats and Shelley.
Shakespeare stands alone.

And I stand lonely, unable to wander, yet just as lonely as any cloud.

Should I rhyme died with pride or cloud with proud?

Alas, I sighed.

At the sweat lodge, we greet the world, "All my relations."
In solitude, I greet the swirling words, please fill my beggar's cup.

I watch the warriors, their whirling swords editing what I write,
until the page is empty. When the saints come marching in,
I long to join the chorus. Is this song or is this weeping?

My beggar's cup is filled with words, lent to me for safekeeping.

X. CODA

Prose: Today in Washington Square Park I saw two hawks
flying in the eastern sky.

Poetry: Today I saw, and knew,
believed, and shivered,
as two hawks performed their ritual dance,
predatory,
as we below,
so unaware,
without a care,
enjoyed eternal youth.
Whose Hand
inked the hawkish pair
against the bright blue summer sky?

Hail to thee, fond Shelley,
bird thou never wert,
"teach me half the gladness that thy brain must know."

You said you were listening now. Ah, you were listening then.

Fond Keats, are you still flying yet
"on the viewless wings of Poesy."
You asked if what you found
were vision or a waking dream,
you ask, "do I wake or sleep?"

Shelley, we weep with you for Adonais,
Shelley, we weep for you.

Lark and nightingale, like mermaids,
will you or won't you sing for me?

Hawk, your scream is green, I want you green….
Cuckoo and dove, ma jolie columbe,
incanting day and night,
you've etched the sky within my heart
and I solemnly swear I will do my part
to sing as if….

APPENDIX

Explication of the terms and references in the poem *A Theory of Influence*

The poem is inspired by the concepts delineated by Harold Bloom in his influential book, *The Anxiety of Influence: A Theory of Poetry.*"

In my poem I chose to honor "all my relations", my literary ancestors.

The poem is divided into ten sections. Six of the ten sections have titles drawn from the titles of six chapters of Bloom's book. Below I define the terms as he uses them, and in some instances meanings other than his intent, but which I use for the poem's sake.

CLINAMEN: Poetic misreading, or misprision proper. Bloom takes the word from Lucretius, who uses it to describe the swerve of atoms. In a sense, the poet creates a new poem to correct the poem of her or his predecessor.

TESSERA: Completion and antithesis. Tessera means tile, a piece of mosaic structure. Bloom takes the term from ancient mystery cults, where the piece of mosaic was used as a token of recognition. The poet recognizes his or her predecessor poet, and in the poet's understanding, completes the work of the predecessor. In my poem, I emphasize the mosaic.

KENOSIS: Bloom takes the term from St. Paul, who uses it to denote an emptying out, a sacrifice, as Jesus emptied and humbled himself by submitting to losing the protection of being divine by becoming human. The poet submits to the predecessor poet, yet the predecessor poet also empties the self. In my poem, I refuse to empty out.

DAEMONIZATION: Bloom defines the term as a movement to a generalized Counter-Sublime, in reaction to the predecessor poet's Sublime. Bloom takes the term from Neo-Platonism, in which a seeker is entered into by an intermediary who has come to help. He applies this to the poet's attitude toward her or his predecessor, a power the poet sees as inherent in poetry itself, but not owing to the predecessor poet. This is a form of identification. The poet identifies with the act of writing poetry, with the poem coming into existence, but not the predecessor poet.

ASKESIS: Self-purgation, culminating in a state of solitude. The poet does not empty out, but the poet limits the self and also limits the predecessor.

APOPHRADES: Return of the dead. The poet holds her or his work open to the predecessor poet, to receive the influence, yet the work is not open, it is held open. Bloom says the impact on the reader is as if the predecessor poet had written the new poem.

REFERENCES:

RECEIVING THE GIFT: Alef, beit, licking honey. Refers to the custom among eastern European Jews of teaching children to read by introducing them to the alphabet by having them lick honey off a coated page, revealing the first few letters, alef, beit, so that learning is sweet.

Other references are to Genesis, the Bible.

Language of the birds: The power to understand the language of the birds signifies great wisdom and mystical ability in European myth, found in ancient Greek and Nordic myth. Also found in Sufism, Kaballah, and other traditions.

SHARING THE GIFT:

Word-music, refers to a book I wrote about the IFPE Poetry Posse

I and Thou, by Martin Buber

Guide for the Perplexed, by Maimonides

CLINAMEN:

Atomopomorphize: word made up by poet, playing off anthropo-morphize, to suggest atoms projecting their qualities onto other entities, such as mathematics and humans

Poets, as the atoms swerve: the formal structure of this verse echoes the formal structure of lines by W. B. Yeats: "Irish poets, learn your trade/sing whatever is well made", from "Under Ben Bulben"

TESSERA:

Begins with a line from the great civil rights anthem, "Lift every voice and sing", lyrics by James Weldon Johnson, music by John Rosamond Johnson. Quotes a line from "Take your place on the great mandala", sung by Peter, Paul, and Mary, written by Mary Travers, Peter Yarrow, Albert B. Grossman

KENOSIS:

Refers to another W.B. Yeats line, "For nothing can be whole or sole...." from "Crazy Jane Talks to the Bishop". The line is "For nothing can be whole or sole that has not been rent", and I added to the line, making it "that has not be torn or rent". In my hubris I sought to improve on Yeats' rhythm. Yeats is my favorite poet – my master.

"Sing, O Muse" refers to Homer and the opening line of the Iliad.

Feeding the multitude and fish become word refers to the story of Jesus feeding the multitudes with a loaf of bread and a fish, and the phrase "And the Word was God", and the religious symbol of the fish representing Jesus.

DAEMONIZATION:

Ahimsa is a Jain greeting, meaning "without violence". Shanti means peace in Sanskrit.

"There is nothing new under the sun" is from Ecclesiastes.

ASKESIS:

Begins with a haiku that refers to Basho's famous haiku of a frog jumping into the water. Is followed by lines from an American Appalachian folk song, "Froggie went a-courting."

The next set of lines draws from many sources:

"You don't miss your water 'til your well runs dry" is an American folk blues.

If mermaids sing, and not to me, refers to T.S. Eliot, "Song of J. Alfred Prufrock".

"Suzanne," poem and song by Leonard Cohen

"Beaded bubbles winking at the brim" from "Ode to a Nightingale" by John Keats

heavenly alchemy, referring to "Gilding pale streams with heavenly alchemy, from Shakespeare's sonnet 33, "Full Many a Glorious Morning I Have Seen"

"After long silence", from the poem by W.B. Yeats, which begins, "Speech, after long silence…."

REFERENCES:

Let there be speech that transcends understanding," referring to Philippians, 4:7, The New Testament, "The peace of God that surpasseth all understanding"

Beggar's cup. A reference to an earlier poem I wrote. I am my own predecessor.

APOPHRADES:

"The Ballad of Joe Hill" by Alfred Hayes and Earl Robinson

"I wander lonely as a cloud" from the poem "I Wandered Lonely as a Cloud" by William Wordsworth

"When the saints come marching in," American gospel hymn, popularized as a Dixieland jazz standard by Louis Armstrong

"All my relations" is a phrase used in sweat lodge rituals by indigenous Americans, the first people

CODA:

"Bird thou never wert," from Percy Bysshe Shelley, "Ode to a Skylark"

"On the viewless wings of Poesy," from John Keats, "Ode to a Nightingale"

"Do I wake or sleep?" from John Keats, "Ode to a Nightingale"

"Adonais", by Shelley, mourning Keats

"I want you green" refers to "Green, how I Want You, Green," by Federico Garcia Lorca

"Jolie columbe," from French folk tune, "Aupres de ma blonde"

PART TWO: WITCHCRAFT AIN'T NOTHING BUT A GOOD WOMAN FEELING BAD

Mother, The Horses Rode

Mother, the horses rode outside my window
All the night long. I could hear their hoof beats
                    ringing clear as silver
I could see their manes a-swirling
                    light and bright as silver.
I could see their wild eyes glowing wet with moonlight.

Something happened in my body.
I am wounded.

Here's the terror and the puzzle:
Sometimes I could hear them running
Hear the clang of rushing hoof beats
Wild and free outside my window
Wild and free and wet with moonlight
As I lay in bed a-trembling
All in wonder at my window
Sometimes I was running with them
Wild and free and wet with moonlight
And my hair was loose and flowing
Silver in the long dark hours.

Hush, my child. Don't tell your father.
        Do not say you heard the horses.

Mother, all night long I wonder
Who I am when I am running
With the horses in the hours
Of the wild and dark free-flowing.

Something happened in my body.

Was I in my bed a-sleeping
Was I silver-maned and fearless
Running moon-mad with the horses.

Hush, my child. The men might listen.
        Do not speak of moons and horses.

Mother, you must answer truly.
When the moon is swallowed and eaten
By the black hawk of the long night
Something happens in my body.
I am wounded.

The hawk draws blood from out my body.
Was I in my bed a-dreaming
Did I run, a mare in moonlight.
I think perhaps I am a witch.

Hush, my child. You rode the night mare.
Rode her silver in the moonlight.

Hear the wind sigh in the pear trees.

Hush, my child. The men might hear us.
                They have fear of women riders
                Who have learned to tame the night mare.

Now I bid you tend the fire.
Stay at home and tend the fire.
Do not speak of night and moon-rides.
Do not speak of hawks and blood.
Do not speak of flight and silver.
Do not speak of dreams and witches.
Do not speak. The men might hear us.
Hush. I bid you tend the fire.

Dreams of a Belly Dancer: I

That my body is a whole world,
That it moves all of a piece
In its many articulations
To the sound of a wolves' chorus:
O the voices of wolves are a blackness
Upon white snows,
Upon unending snows.

I dance because I am beautiful
and there is music.
Because in my old age, black-skirted
and hideous, I will shock the brides
with my knowledge of the ways of men.

The ways of men. They are simple,

These ones, obsessed with strength,

Timid in the face of something other.

Old, I will frighten them,

Lifting my skirt to betray the stinking

Of my flesh and juices.

But now I dance for the sound

Of the sun, of gold and pearls upon the shape

Of me.

Dreams of a Belly Dancer: II

The stage is set:
Boy! Yes, you,
You with the drum,
Set the beat!
The singer starts to sing and all is still.

My body is a harp slung on a fig tree,
And I am the wind that set the harp strings stirring
As I move to the sound of your heavy listening
I am the gold and glory of your captured breath.

Women are all the same.
Another roll of the hips, old men, another
Throw of the dice;
The wheel of a body turning , turning slow,
Boys, the interstice
Between passion and game.

And I am slow and cool as blood from an old wound
For I followed the tracks of an escaping moon
Through the forest paths at night
And I learned her moves and dodges, men,
I learned her ways.

The finger cymbals know a grandmothers' song.
The singer's mouth is blood and silence:
Now the old bacchantes in the corner moan,
They click their hands full of worn bones,
And they are waiting, boys,
They've waited long.
They are hard
And naked in their age beneath their veils.

For my mother's a witch and she lives by the sea
And she's always a-telling her lies to me
My father's a fisherman, lives all alone
He makes his dinner
On a chewed-down bone.

The grandmothers sing:
We're tracking the young boys to their lairs
Though they travel alone, though they prowl in pairs
There's nothing can set these young boys free
But dawn and the death of the wind-blown fig tree.

The harp;
The rattle of bones;
The turning of the body:

The dancer is impaled by eyes.

This Appears to be a Desert

These places lie like salt upon the tongue,
these minor travelings, dry as death.
I did not want to come here, made no
arrangements, did not expect to be alone.
This appears to be a desert:
There are no oranges here!
Give back the blood of things!
For here there is sand in all the clocks;
machinery clanks and whistles along the spine.

There are limping dogs in the market,
blue flies in the hanging gardens,
sand in my shoes,
frogs in the bed.

Some one else has cheated at cards; I
stack the tarot pack to where it must tell lies.
O! I call down all the great houses, I whistle
at sea. God calls up from smoking crevices,
wheezing like a goat. We throw the young ones down
and turn away. Tomorrow some one else will poison the well,
and cry the hours of the night until the sands spell day.

Fields of Wheat

But come O you mourning women,
you in your girlhoods, you
like fields of wheat,
keep close to the color of your doors.
O do not dance, do not sorrow
among the shackled sheaves.

Wait. Heroes will come to rescue you
from fields of wheat in the yellow of day.
Heroes will rescue you from your mothers.
You will cross great sheets of grey water.
You will forget, who cannot remember to mourn.

What sound is this, this great humming of bees,
this thrumming of metal strings,
like the mouth of a harp?
You are dead, your daughters' daughters are dead,
your bones are returned into forest and swamp,
into fields of ripe wheat,
and your sorrow is still drumming.

There comes a priest with breasts,
priest with mad hair and shrieking spade.
She uncovers the song of your bones,
she is uncovering the long silence of earth.

Fair Game

In games of chance
we dream of chase;
blood barks at the dog in the moon.

Yonder comes some fallow doe
as heavy with young as she may go:
fair game. For the sorb-apple
is in season, and the nightingale
sings like an iron engine,
pumping delight.

Those who carry weapons are called warriors.
They have spread romance raw upon a table,
spread her legs and made a mess
with their rough and ready butcher's way.

The crab and the jackal
fight for the tender parts.

The nightingale, wired for sound,
trills all the latest hits.
The bones of a deer, worn soft as rotting leaves,
keep interpreting back to the earth
the meaning of the changes
of the calling of the wind.

Elegy

for Elena

The ruins of the moon shatter
upon your bedroom floor.
Night-blooming flowers, sap rising,
freeze in a blue enamel pitcher:
rumpled fossil of your body within moist and empty sheets,
bottles labeled medicine, still rolling,
among splinters of moonlight
and you, with your face like a marble slab
and heart mad as the last lap of a thoroughbred winner,
You, dropping through the beach
into the belly of the ocean
like a pure and breathless blade.

We hear about another suicide and we grow uneasy
as if some drunk sat next to us in the subway
as if some man we knew but didn't much care for
started removing all his clothes at a party
as if some stranger stared at us too long
as if some nightclub singer forgot the words to her song.

Do we forget what it is makes us grow uneasy?
(We hear about another suicide.)
Our friend, this woman, a poet, up and died
as if by her own free will and grace,
pretending –

Weep O weep all you women O weep
She is dead who might have written your stories.
O you women weep.

The Miracle of the Mirror

Give me a mirror for my name –

I see the snake in the eye of the bird.
When skin and shadows creep
the sun flames its little death
and wild with grief the women weep.

Give me a mirror for my name –

She has birthed a monster,
some twisted thing. Wolves
discover the singing of blood
in her hair. And her spine
is on fire, among the water lilies,
with her hair drowning as wolves
discover a pathway shifting from hip to hip,
like a whore, to where some twisted thing
is floating raw among the weeds.
Her lungs are a chalice, bubbling
with something hot and sticky, something like blood.

Something gone has broken:
Give me a mirror for my name –

Lamentations of the wild swans,
at winter, among black branches,
cries as white as stone against the moon.

Song for Terry

Terry says she was just another
Gangling New England Teenager
the day she took the rowboat out to sea.
I see it all in black and white:
a photograph of 1956.
She wore rumpled cotton shorts
and a sleeveless blouse with peter pan collar,
and her feet were fourteen years old and bare.
But her hair! was caught suddenly behind and then
flowed free. That was the year she stumbled
over a wave and fell into a yacht,
into the rich folks' floating yard.

The movie script says here they were all so rich
and brilliant and decadent and grotesque,
drinking champagne and thinking poetry.
For the women wore diamonds and the men wore gold,
and all were young and none were old,
and one had a hunchback and flippers for arms,
another no nose and another webbed hands.
They fed her ticklish wine and smiled at her freckles,
and sang strange rhymes spiced with dark hashish.

Terry says she was just another summer and fifteen
and up to her shoulders in hotel dishwater
earning her future on the breast of labor.
She bound crinkled dollar bills into bouquets
tied with red ribbon and sweet with sachet
and bought dresses.

White and pink and blue she bought them
stiff with crinoline, spangled with rhinestones,
tart as taffeta and sugared as lace,
and five pounds of cold cream to smother her face
to have all the dreams of the world in her closets.
Heavy with brass rings her fingers,
burdened with plaster pearls her shoulders,
fastened round with gilt her wrists,
heaving beneath paste jewels her bosom,
and fair as meadow-rushes her just-loosened hair.
Out into the island fields she brought them,
into one dress and out again she shimmered,
lost in the long grasses of Maine.
Her mother took snapshots
in 1957
that later the whole world would know
the heaven of dresses woven of newsreel
fracturing the hollywood heart.

Saturday, August, the town has gone dusty,
has sagged in the middle, smells of spilled Pepsi,
fat in the last green growth of summer.
Terry first painted her cheeks, lips, and eyelids
with pom-pom pink lipstick and June-sky blue shadow.
In her best party dress Terry honored the mirror,
fastened her ribbons and rustled her silks,
drank a brown bottle of sweetened cough syrup,
headed downtown in high heels and blue gown.
Floated for hours, a cinema princess.
Choked in her dream in the back seat of a car.

I am singing this song for Terry to answer;
I am writing this movie and Terry's the star:
On a yacht in the ocean a fairy tale princess
flew like a swallow between waves and sky,
flew like a swallow and never turned back.

For Lee

For Lee:

Whose mother wore white gloves
when she beat her little girl:

With wind and waves like a grey night in her eyes;
those eyes, horizon-colored.
Lee, in pillbox hat and veil,
spending every long young year
like small change
upon train fare.

Girlhood unwinds from her
like a long velvet ribbon,
black as regret.
They have pawned her dowry;
things whispered around the corners
of her tight house.

It's like falling from a still merry-go-round
into the heart of concrete,
one second at a time.

Lee comes sweeping into the big town,
wrapped around her cape,
looking for the long lean free time,
after losing every one of her spare change.

Coming Home by Way of Louisville, Kentucky

for Al, a Black Man who was a Colored Boy

Walking the alleys
and vacant lots
of Al's childhood,
I find window glass
smudged with fingerprints
of all those others
peeking out at me.

I am not patient
with my own steps
skipping past
past me.

He took my hand with
crayon to draw his
childworld, and I
walking the alleys
and vacant lots
of memorable names
and living faces

flowering from
dying bodies
could not find
the hiding
of where I used to be.

They built
a house
under the hill
where I,
just once, was
King of the Mountain.

One hard sunlight
day, the alleyway
cool and darker
Marilyn, Ronnie, Annie, Channa-Rifke
confessed a same dream.

Of all the streets
in Brooklyn
settling deeper into
the arms of the planet
there was one with

one apartment house,
one colored man:
he was the superintendant.

And the windows of little girls lay close to the ground.
Dreaming girls, who learned what I never would learn,
who learned excitement from hatred, fears, and lies —

They dreamed
the colored super would
whisper like a nightwind
past ruffled pink
greying at night
into curtains for the center stage,
and from those girls I first heard the word
Rape.

Collectively dreamed
in the cool sanctuary
between houses
staring window to window
at each other's
soft bedroom.

Marilyn never married
anyone. She dreamed
again a definite
spinster spider
secretary's summer cruise
that Hawaiian men
love
fat women.

And Channa-Rifka
grew white lips
white hair white
eyes. Never
married anyone.
Like a Sabbath
candle, she is
kindled
only by
women.

Ronnie married
some one.

Annie some one
married.

Their dreams now irrelevant —
except to me —

Their molten dream like
the pure piss-gold of alley puddles
eaten by concrete.

It seemed to me they
wanted him to
the first hard
sunlight
I heard
in the cool and darker alley
the word
Rape.

Al keeps saying it was like Bedlam,
there,
in Louisville,
Kentucky.

In Tilden Lot
there was a valley
as lost as Solomon's
Mines. A girl
could not see over
the mountains the
street. A small
girl.

4:30 in the afternoon
         after
a white boy from the high school
a boy as big as a man
took me to see the puppies in
Tilden Lot.

Puppies wet as birth
in a nest of leaves.

Not here. Further.
    Deeper.
    Where it is most still.

As alone
as a small girl could not see over

the mountains the
street.

Not here.
    Here.

Where his fly unzippered he showed her
puppies wet as birth
in a nest of leaves.

She will never believe in the miracle of birth.

Beyond my night window
on Saturday night
the boys from the high school
take the girls from the high school
down the pizza arcade
and instead of sharing dreams
with open-eyed bedrooms
I watch their laughter
especially the Italian boys
sleeker and harder than alley cats.

They built a junior high school
                on Tilden Lot

crushing the mountains
that sheltered puppies wet as birth
nested and lost as Solomon's mines.

                                    Seven and seven
                                    and I was fourteen
                                    in the pizza arcade.
                                    Sleeker and harder than
anything. We all could add seven and seven in sips.
I liked the one who said he had killed a man. My cowboy hat,
charcoal and pink, a felt orchid.
There is nothing to remember but
                                    further
                                            deeper
where it is most still.

Al keeps saying it was insanity,
there,
in Louisville,
Kentucky.

It was peaceful and still on the streets,
coming home, past molten piss-gold dreams,
by way of Tilden Lot, by accident....

I Demanded of the Witch

I demanded of the witch
that she weave my dreams into meaning
her fingers stumbled in the dark
and changed the story.

Three gifts she gave me:
Fire plaited into my hair
a handful of sand
sunset visions.

Fire: I blinded three men
                     and burned my bridges

Sand: I stopped the ticking of my heart
                     murdered my need for tears
                     found food for beggar children

Visions at sunset: I did not die. I would never die.

O Witch in the Doorway
troubled by laughter
fingers darting yellow like cat's eyes
body angled like a house all tumble-down
incantations mad with words like runaway mice
and her laughter like night,
dark and silent.

Three times she swept her doorstep clean
Three times she shrieked out all her windows
Three times she fondled secret things
Before bat-wings took hold of her broom
and flew her.

The last I saw she was beating the moon
and twisting her voice into a chill wind
the last I saw she was raking the stars
before the huntsman slew her.

He cried: I saw a swan and shot her.
He cried: I saw a deer and killed her.
He said: I dreamed a shadow among the trees,
                  something not quite there

And when I loosed the arrow
I heard the thumping of a heart throughout the land
and then I heard a silence.

I bound him to me by the hairs of my head
stuffed sand in his bread and told him lies.
And when his dreams turned sour and mean
I spilled his riddles in a stony stream.

Now the witch Is dead and the huntsman is blind
and the moon is rotting in a naked sky
and the doorway is locked and the broom is asleep
and the house in the forest is afraid of the dark.

I demanded of the witch
that she weave my dreams into meaning
her fingers tangled and broke the thread
and the rest –

      the rest –

           is story.

Poor Boy and The Witch: A Space Duet

What it was the witch forgot,
What in the world the witch forgot –

I spin, I spin
I spin thrice round
Within this dance he is bound,

                              poor boy.

What is it we stir
that bubbles and brews, what
is it we stir?
Throw something in.
It comes to the static limit,
it enters the radial dragging
where no light gets out,
here, in this tight spot,
this black hole,
this witches' pot.

I spin, I spin

I spin thrice round

Close, close to snare a man like a moth on a pin,

                              poor boy

The moon so full she causes ovaries to wince and tighten,

the moon so full she causes blood to flow,

the womb to lighten,

the heart to narrow.

He lingers at the event horizon

as if he were hitching a ride.

Watching the traffic along the particle path,

this poor boy encountered a singularity;

O do not say he died.

Rather, he reached an absolute limit of math.

I spin, I spin

I spin thrice round

I keep whatever it is I've found,

                              poor boy.

What it was the witch forgot,

what in the world the witch forgot –

Answers

O mommy.
Where are the answers
you embroidered into my hands
like starshine at noon,
invisible and bright
a silver spoon unravelling.

I stood so still
a long winter's night
my palms blinded upon the warmth
of a tinker's fire.

Where is the little man
who taught me to clap my hands in the dark,
to make noise like music
within a tent of sinew and flesh.
Who is the little dark man
who pierced my ankles
with the jawbone of an ass
and wove jewels into the empty wounds.

Who is the cockroach gnawing
at the razor nicks on knuckles and thumb.
In a nest of crumpled tissues
girl-babies and mice lie tangled and complete.
A silver canoe, a birchbark thimble, a gift
of some worth: glass beads and paper hankies.
Some gypsy technocrat owns this part of the forest.

O mommy.
Where are the answers
the tongue-man stole into his green
wheelbarrow, answers pasted like first-grade stars
into the alley, between windows of mute lust.
Where are the violent dogs
and all the muscular games of skill.

My teachers rustle about like bats
and leave me back a century.
Cities squat in the graveyard;
finders keepers.

Look. I am compelled by the sea,
I patrol this strand.
I pay attention to the whisperings within shells,
I am wet, metallic, splashed with scales,

reduced to the glint of moonlight
buried in the sand.

Look. I am neither mermaid nor ragged claw,
nor served up raw upon the half shell.
The horizon is a cave; the sun is a bat.
These test questions are all wrong.
Your answers are a simple song,
now what do you think of that?

Don't lie to me.
I have walked on fire, and all I learned
is if I cried, I would be burned.
I could have wept, I might have screamed.
You hoped I slept, you claimed I dreamed.

The tinker kept a little tent
of prayer among his fingers.
I clapped my hands and prayed for rain.
The answers fell with a crash,
like cherry petals upon the grass.

Lightning has forced me toward silence,
pale as a stone.
Remember how I stitched beginnings and endings of stories
between forefinger and thumb, and blew them away?
The fire claimed then I had nothing to say.

I wish a grey mare would rise up from the sea
and trample the earth into ashes.

Awakening

Smoke uncurling: cat/soul/fire
drifting dark sea eastern sun
myself a fish
dragged toward air and light
in another's net

Lies

The lines of my face tell lies.
I have never suffered.
The rose is red beyond my eyes.

Exploration and Other Abortions

Each delving into earth discovers
Ruin. Among the jags and edges
These severed heads, of pure
And noble stone, thrown casually,
Promiscuously, towards a kiss.

Here there is accident, there are
Great expectations. In these
Amphitheaters are the forms of god
Shattered and compelled to touch
As if by love
For aristocratic appetite.

Among the earth-spattered mouths
Of bruised and fortuitous lovers
Are pathways left for soldiers
Who march, always, among
Continual forgotten ruins.

When the great forest recoiled from the presence of blood
We disemboweled our mother; from her cords and bones
Erected cities. In each spattering of water

Hides a mirror; with every turning away of
Eye from eye the conspiracy
Of common death. The flowers shrink from women;
These decays of roses the delusion of pleasure.

These are our hands; they die of the shape
of blood, they wither at the touch
of simple flowers.

Motion is the only illusion

There are those who cannot be named:
They have felt the beating heart of a small bird
in the pulses of their weak, their weakest fingers
truly in rhythm the flattening of dimension
the wholing of apposite and boundaried pieces

Fracturing is the whole intent
and further words that signify
Destruction
are totally
inaccurate

The Body of Eve

I no longer believe that the Bible is true:
how do men really feel about childbirth?

Magic whispers from the fingertips of menstruous women,
and the tree-top voices of warrior boys
are clogged with shame.
That Bible ain't religion, honey, it is our culture
and we are all true believers.

Eve, she always gets hers! A naked goddess among the serpents,
she commanded twin fruits of a tree that flowered
around and through her living body: and grandpa got so mad!
Sorrowful childbirth and a man for a master
is what she got for being so uppity,
that independent goddess with a mind all her own.
How do men really feel about childbirth?
How do women really feel about women?
Who is more sacred than I?

I will dance right into the sky and bind the earth with my hair,
I will harvest stars like answers, wash clean the face of the moon,
I will herd clouds into the corrals of the mountains,

O I will delight in the green feathers of grass along the road.
Every bird that flies will chant my name and every morning
I will rise up born again into this body
and who is more sacred than I?

Mapmaker

It is not my religion to receive wounds.
The dictionary discovers accident.
I discover the contour of the sea
Where the shore must be.

The landmarks of my body have grown
Familiar, are changing with the sea tides.
My face is worn and golden as the moon.
This scar upon my knee, the mark of lightning.
I was once a tree felled by a man's hand.
This spider web upon my belly, geological
Upheaval. Ancient history.
Read me like a book.

I am grown denser. You can't slip through
Any more. I am nobody's ghost.
At most I am a tower in a desert of black sands,
At most I am the shape of something darker than the night
You stumble across when fleeing from your dreams.
At least today I am feeling so much better.

It is not my religion to receive wounds.
This is only a body.

The River Nymph Sings of Treasure

The skeleton of a ship. So what?
The young sailors, the old, all dead.
The miller's daughter drowned.
Young girls come down to the river every year,
to search for water between the banks.
To see faces of flowers flow down to the sea.
To throw gold to sailors, the young, the old,
all dead.

The fragments of this shattered skull.
If I put it back together, would it be an egg?
Do I win a prize?
All poems are questions, all propositions
have shadows, all thinking is echo,
is echo – – –

Poems and problems: solve me.

Remember me.

Sing the sound of me.

String my hair to my breastbone, for I would be a harp.

The river sang the song of my life from the river

I was born.

Throw back the bones.

Maiden

I have seen
I have come closer
drawn by a promise
in and of decay.

We agree, conditionally,
on simulated memory.

Where, in which dark,
did we become, unalterably,
Snake?
Mating in which crevice,
which yielding upholstery,
with a hiss and a shedding of skins....

We cannot bear that it can be so.
We lie:
We are not snakes,
and our childhood is not in ruins;
the angel at the garden gate
lets fall the sword,
invites us home.

Out of Phase

Blood is weeping, weeping in the body:

Past

We learn to walk around small
grinning threat, keeping our balance.
The surface of the world glinted with teeth,
with sharpened flames; places to stumble,
places to fall. We crouched back down
to where we were born, unable to hide.

Present

We compile a list of impossibilities, keep a steady beat:
    We cannot drink sand.
    We cannot breathe glass.
    We cannot walk upright in the sun.
    We cannot be born except in shadow.
    We cannot bury danger and not bleed.

Future

We are going to learn to appreciate the contours
of our accidental deaths. We will develop
an eye for detail. Sand will absorb
our running steps, our little wet spatters,
our signs of civilization, our shaping of sleep.

Resolve

This moment, accidental, impossible,
full of grace, is being trampled
by thirsty feet. Sands bleed
between our toes, and we think
we are satisfied, we dream
we are re-born.

Time Test

In   com   plete bridge
hiatus
I walk across a bridge
I stop
at the hiatus
I (can, could) easily leap to the shore
I walk back across the bridge
I am walking across the bridge
I walked across the bridge
I have walked across the bridge
I have always walked across the bridge
I am always walking across the bridge
I walk always across the bridge
I walk, always, across the bridge
What of the future?
Conditional.
Describe the relationship (between, among)
hiatus and time.

Webs We Weave

I: INSECT PORNOGRAPHY

Balance this equation:

INSECT   pornography
insect   HELL

don't stop please don't stop I don't want it ever
to stop

STOP

these two thinking they are lovers
embrace, immobile, in the slight
shimmer of karmic web
woven by a spider god –

a spider god who went away,
who later died.

These two
are lovers and hang drying
in the air, suspended against rock.
No one heard their moans or saw their sufferings:
they were not even eaten.

a poet (may have) killed a spider
a poet turned away from a rock

this time and space, this interstice,
this web, is more b-e-a-u-t-i-f-u-l
to the poet
                    than is the struggle
but is not, therefore, any more
REAL.

II: INSECT RITUAL

Terror
Again

        I return to a sacred place
and find a spider as big as the universe
in my path

I am afraid of webs so fine,
so thin, that (i) can break

approaching the temple tree
another web
o airborne lovers
a trap
that from itself a spider spins
out of hunger

i think i am dying now
therefore i cannot deal with anything

       Terror

       Again

spider web
broken glass in a subway car window
follows me

III: LIBERATION

Along the path of the mindshape lake
at the gateway to the shrine of himalayan larch
in the dissolve of: sun shadow wind water

SUDDENLY:

it

it already happened

it happened

it is done

Captured by the spider's web
I destroyed it and was set free.
because of my carelessness, my fright, my rage,
the small deaths of possible insects
are averted
for this short while

I do not care whether a spider feasts
or a fly escapes

Tell me, o wanderers of this earth
Who was it set me free?

Japanese Garden 1975

designed by Takeo Shiota for
the Brooklyn Botanic Garden

It is Brooklyn now.
Poetry is already here.
Takeo Shiota unified elements.

Lake flows in mindshape.

eternal	object
spirit	bamboo
time	rock
life	pine

Takeo Shiota
we
who are here

The presence of a nearby shrine.

Great
Illuminating
Deity

Unity

G   W
A   A
T   Y
E

It is Brooklyn in my mindshape.
I have always been – this –

It is easy to honor sun
here.
Garden is across lake
West of our eyes
Birds dance sunset
in trees that verge on mindshape
West of our eyes
the sun here
is honored

It is easy to honor water
here
for ducks summer here
in perpetual foodsquabble
in families
in mating dyad
in formation
and bullfrogs discover the voice
of hidden, soft, evening grasses
albino carp and flitting minnows
a deep and dusty green
are seen
where bread is cast upon the waters
here

Air alive
with change
Sunset into evenings
flight into nest
breath into rest
Gold to night

Water steps
    like stepping stones
        down
            its own
        fall
and is itself
sound within caverns
    stepping stones
        lift skirts
        to cross
        water
    like weeping trees
            lower
        towards the glass
            skin
        between
air and water
    knows

whenever "i" walk upon the paths
    one stops to feel with hands with skin
membrane of cypress
    hairy and smooth

Clarity (Botanic Gardens of Brooklyn)

Things retain their ancient form.

These pines do not care
which centuries, which cultures
are synchronous
with their being –

when meanings are deciphered
the answers are not formed
with words.

The heart intuits
what it has always
known –

     these black, these twisted
trees, these eccentricities
of shape against an eternal
sky; at dusk, already
sumi-e

Shatterings

$A = {\sim}A$
if it is real it is not real

There is not this way to approach this problem:
words break against the edges of mists
$A > {\sim}A$

I am about to die this second time.
Counting is an original sin.

Where there is no number there is no pain.

I am a diagram of a body.

We will number where the soul variously be:
So begin the chronicle of openings,
the numberings of pain.
There are seven chakras,
seven births, seven
ruptured fantasies:

Survival, union, power,
compassion, god, wisdom,
the ineffable habitually conceived
as light....

Here balance is mangled
and in the absence of connections
severed parts present a unity of function.

Alternatives offer only
the monotony of change...
if it is real, it is not whole
if it is real, it is whole;
seamed, fissured, gaping, broken

it is real

therefore

Magic is a whole thing
Faith moves where there is no other change
in interlocking symmetries
in spherical direction

It is only in the breaking of flesh
that we are comprehended by the real
tearing through another to be born
to be born to be torn
Magic is a whole thing
a blind thing
a stone

the miracle is that we are torn
and therefore live

that we are comprehended by the real
a blind, a magic thing
a stone

Puzzle

I

My hands have grown translucent in the dark.
Along the narrow lifeline a frog's heart pumps thick blood
Through narrow veins. My hands become dry oak leaves,
and rustle, dry and papery, falling to the autumn floor.
A pulse has stopped.
I hear its silence.
Two mice dance blindly at my feet,
Climb up my legs, and disappear.
My wrists bleed autumn sap upon the rug,
Carrying the rhythm, and then applaud.
The dark has turned translucent in my hands.

II

I waken in the dark as in a dream.
Collide with what is not as it might seem.
I hear my feet go slither on the floor.
They kick aside what might have been the door.
My dream continues sleeping as before.

III

My eyes, two blind white moths, beat at the walls;
Moonlight hides them.
Candlelight is hiding in the dark.
The walls beat back my eyes.
Each shadow lingers in surprise
At being locked in chunks of space.
Each shadow has the shape of my own face.
The window, capturing the moon, lies still and dead.

IV

In the morning a seamstress threads her way
Alone to where the parts of me begin.
She chalks the print of night into my skin
And stitches past the skeleton of the moon.
It's early; she has come too soon.
The sun explodes, at war with day.

V

There is a fire in the night.
There is a fire in the night.
There is a fire.
In the night.

VI

The wind and trees must trust relationship.
I am a body fluttered by their sad embrace.
Shadow and light vie for the bones of me.
The moon swallows the dawn.
The last I see
Is the fatal disappearance of the sun.

Future Shock

I went to see the fortune teller.

Like any Gemini, she can only be proud
of her contradictions. She is six feet tall,
this woman, in the right shoes. She can be
six feet tall when she needs to be.
Her voice is a slender oboe, a reed
in a low grey wind, a speaking cavern.
And her hair is yellow, like her fawn years,
yellow as girlhood, a whisper of gold
in the stolid bedrock of time.
Her grandmother made soap of rooster heads
in an iron cauldron. She keeps her
eyes in a white pine box,
Gemini stars.

She read

my journey, my wheel of days

in picture cards.

My epitaph is my chart.

I am a lion, I am a living queen,

and I shall have a sweet death.

All my choices are in the house of mystery:

Should I live existentially,

all my doings would surprise me.

Mind Country

The landscape of where
it all happened
stained blue and sea
and green, a mirror
wet and wavering.

Keep rearranging the furniture
of the stone bedroom
as
the old established form clings to the walls
souvenirs of who

In a glass vial are moldering the annotated hairs
of those who used my brush and comb
in the morning.

Moldering into soft old dust
a living constant
that all must die

Flies swarm thickest
round the craziest eyes
in the photo-finish gallery

Mustangs run against gravity
this darkest night of the stellar year,
trampling sleep.

Some pale moon wonder woman
lets loose her trembling hair
to coax the wanton willow to weep
to make a pretty picture for the yearbook

This is where god autographed my soul,
Here. And here is where god's pride
must fall. And here is where
the wild goes free. And here
is where the want must be.

Most reluctant guide

Landscape is painted
in a wash of schizophrenic
colors coming true

A starless night is truer still,
promising, as always,
Nothing

Voice of No

March and September are
space of a moon probe
to become
Crazy

You know Crazy

Everybody know
Crazy

Like dreaming he is
cream sherry and i drink of him to get high
but his eyes expanding
eat me through the soul

i wonder
how his eyes expanding
so inside me
see and out like that
like the full moon being all
all day and all night all
hard

if i be possessed by scream
and other manifestations
i quest some odd place of me i have not found
to hide

the shape of laughter
sometimes
       is the shape of
          some minor readjustment
      as well as structural calamity
            integrated into new modes

new moon
in false sky

we want to catch apocalypse at the beginning
because the plot counts

to understand
everybody
know
Crazy

like everybody know it all

If

The last time
the words were plain
like words as seeds
within the brain:
a rain forest
of beasts and flowers.

The last time
I said, simple,
like this:
If
there is nothing
special between us
then
there is nothing
between us.

SPECIAL
Your eyes closed
your child eyes
closed for surprise
and golden the O! of your mouth.

I am dust everywhere in your world
in the gutters wet with rain, grape soda rain
pollen and rotten leaves and dog shit –

You will seek in rainbow plate glass longing
among the women's shoes
and Miller's High Life
my name.

My name
is patterned with the stars
as name
among all scattered
Daily News
women's shoes
store front lyric
blue satiric
Name

Here I am
writing on the wall
I am
my name on the wall
my gang name
my street

IF

on the wall
off the wall

Here I am
too fast past
your child eyes

My subway name
lost at Times Suare
pink and gold
I told
my real name to your eyes
surprise
and gone

If
there is nothing
not your eyes
golden as your mouth
between us
then
there is nothing
a shattered fuck of a paste-pearl lily-gilded night
between us.

I too can see what you can see
it's all a matter of timing
in rhyming
couplets
and there is nothing
different
between us

This time
I say the words for real
I feel
only with my skin

The last world I was living
was not the world
I am in

These words are not a poem
except for you
in my words

this time I try to tell you
I found my name
written in the stars
of last night's morning

A Simple Song
Yeshiva voice
a sunshine ribbon through
the simple of it:
You grope about
the whole of it
to touch components
which you understand.
Triumphant song.
You, a bull swan,
rejoicing by rote.
Your eyes smile away
from my seeing:
Women are so simple.

I am betrayed by
your voice. I can
not choose not
to understand.

Men are so simple
it hurts.

Clocktalk

There were sweet times gone
by, we say, justifying
if not memory then faith.
How could I have come to
this moment so alone, with
no time as force? How
could I have come so
alone to this moment, with
no other as guide? Yet
here this moment and this
lone commingle, here I
am. There is no rustle
of familiarity,
clocktime meshes with
the rev of motor from
a frightened truck,
mechanical tick and roar.
A sparrow feathers cold
away on a link of fire
escape; it will not know
me. This world that
leaks into absurdity

was a pattern only yesterday: I
was an atom in the mind
of god. Today I feel
myself, and find I
have no feelings. Such
a morning, without
pity, hard against
my skin. Such
a morning, smogged
with sunlight pattern,
brick and metal
an abstraction
that speeds away
from center.
The spaces on
the clock claim it
is time: but
I don't know
why.

Say What

ever-becoming
mythic you
accuses me
of becoming
succubus
of incubi

Before and After the War

We move toward the abstract as the result of terror:

Finding in the city some minor celebration of a dead war.
I crouch on the ground among the poets,
Fingering at curbside the counterpoints of cloud and curve.
We watch the traffic remnants weave and hum
An awkward accidental marching song.
Painted shells of steel obey a strict command of colored light –
If I turn my back the forest will reclaim us.

Quiet in our bones among sharp shadows
Hunted by flightless eagles poised in fluted stone
We take the ghosts of Greece and Rome for granted.

Childhood echoes in the noise of alleyways and art and silence
As we remember echo as in childhood.

Why do we delight in shadows and echoes
                              shadows and echoes
                                    shadows and echoes

We live in the center of soft smudges, firm foundation, small

contradiction.

We live at the edges of hard, among the bright crisp dark.

Knocking at the gate in moonlight: it is a long time past
Before the gate is found:
It is a long time found before the knock is answered.
We unravel a thread of fire.

O that I might retreat from my movies and dreams
And paint poems at my window
Where under darkness spirits loom larger than mountains
And dance among deserted city streets,
That I might share the world with hand and eye and tongue and ink.

It was in the city that I was born –
Enamored of the rose I did not mind the thorn.

Looking for Looking at

Stars are
So to see
The nothing
Better
Teaching by light touch
A wholeness of night
Like a place for all to be
While stars are seeking us

When Drunk, or Dreaming...

When drunk, or dreaming, or in poetry
I find you, luminous, as young as when we met
that first green spring of springs
in the time of cherry blossoms
I find you as you were
when all the world was young as spring
as young as we were, then.

When drunk, or dreaming, or in poetry
I find you among all mists and words
isolate
in crumbling air
then I remember yet the glass
between the faces that you wore
the taste of all souls eve like smoke
within your hair.

The death of sunlight in your ageless eyes.

The crumpled skins of paper crackling
like a fire
autumn air about to burst into flame

the twist of spider tree revealed
a summer glory torn to rags
by cold
strict cloud-grey stones
in hardening fields
wet with blood pale as weak pekoe tea.

Something was dying, there, among
the spiky diagram of grasses,
there among the old song of our flesh
black and scorched where first we met.

I heard you play the flute on Second Street:
one of us was drunk
and one of us was dreaming
and one of us was dancing
on Second Street
among the poetry

Office on Second Street: Word-Drunk

The evening empties, a bottle of wine drained too soon,
A last liquid rose splashed between the western sky and night.
And I, drunk at end of day, cling to the puddled gold
Spilling through the wide-eyed windows of my neighbors
As all houses, brick by brick, flash dazzle back to the sun.

And I, drunk at end of day, can no longer keep quiet at my desk,
But shout for the last drop of light to pierce me at the eye,
And sing sober sonnets and modest minuets instead of seeing
Past the leaden dusk. I will not have night and here it is,
Darkening at my window, at my desk, in my dream. I thought
I would never see the sun go down. Don't lie to me about dawn.

I knew nothing once upon a time. The trees believe in their own
Interfacing of green and radiance all through the cold dark
Night. I can smell them still and breathing past the limit
Of the window. The reeling leaves, the sap like wine within,.
The evening empties, a bottle drained too soon. Pale spring
Moon. A final crimson screams and struggles and fades.
I am drunk at end of day, listening to the trees
Keep secrets in the ripening air.

Dialogue to the First Power

Dialogue

CHILD: Is it true, Mother Kali, that karma is function of time?

KALI: What is the function of a question?

CHILD: I thought you had all the answers.

KALI: You think too much.

"I" accumulate.

"I" accumulates.

Philosophy quiz:

The destruction of the universe is

    a) a priori

    b) a posteriori

    c) to what?

To what?

    a) this universe

    b) that universe

    c) to what?

to the second power
DEVI: O Shiva, what is your reality?
SHIVA: Radiant One... be included...

Love quiz:
    a) did you like it?
    b) was it good?
    c) did you hear:
        a) bells
        b) silence
    d) did you feel:
        a) earthquake
        b) stillness
    e) was there an OTHER?

Destroyer, protect "me"
Protector, destroy "me"

This is not a test   repeat   this is not a test
one
two
three
ten thousand
one

"ceaseless binary accuracy"

a thinking computer is a mathematical impossibility

"I" am (that I am) a mathematical impossibility

a poet is writing: this world
Euclid sketches our portrait

God is this small, this small drum

Memories of Dying

Memories of dying are nobody's business.
Mind your own.

1) First: I went blind. Slowly. Through
a thicket of years. This rare radiant
jewel, vision, diminished.
I stalked the subtlety of sight.
"What did I see yesterday that I no longer see
                    today?"
"Are these shadows or remnants of light?"
"What was it I last saw?"
"What did I see last?"
                    First
I went blind.

2) I learned to listen.
Then I went deaf.
Slowly.

3) I learned to smell and taste and touch. Soon,
only touch was. I touched out into the world,
I crawled my skin against all of experience,
I turned inside out.

I felt everything.

4) At last
I went untouching
      untouched
      touchless
      numb

5) Destroy   my   consciousness
   Destroy   my   consciousness
   Destroy   my   consciousness

I am riddles and games and memories
      purity
revelations of a formal grace

all my labyrinths resolve into
      dead end

6) Destroy   my   consciousness

     Destroy   my   consciousness

     Destroy   my   consciousness

7) Conceive me.

     Give birth to me.

     Make me be; make me be conscious.

Survival Kit

The instructions:

1) Do not see things as you have always seen them
Assumptions come gift wrapped in whispers,
that you will see things as they are

the student understands
that she never has

she tried to call
the cobra stared down the sound

all connections are now broken
repeat
all connections are now broken
                              broken
                              broken

she moves away from her last self
like a ship from the slip

is that, she asks, what you mean?

Instructions remain static, silent until
there are no words left
they will mean what they mean
at any level one chooses
to choose

the instructions continue

2) do not see things

From a Teacher's Notebook: Surprise Quiz

1) Who is that person over there?

   a) a sex maniac

   b) a business practitioner

   c) a loving and giving happy person

2) This is a person. What is this person doing?

   a) dancing

   b) curing a sick child

3) This is a person. What is this person doing?

   a) torturing another person

   b) saving another person's life

   c) a job

4) This is a person. What is this person doing?

   a) torturing another person

   b) saving another person's soul

   c) a job

5) What are most of the objects in this room?
   a) nouns: names of persons, places, things
   b) screens to keep the shadows from taking over
   c) distractions from reality

6) What beings are there in this room?
   a) human beings
   b) machine beings
   c) invaders from an alien planet
   d) angels, fairies, demons, ghosts
   e) luminous beings

The Kitchen

What should I think? What should I feel?
Answers are documented in other lives.
All others are examples, and I
am possessed by choice.

What is the value of this?
Help yourself, sir. Another
slice of life? Have we
the measure of our days,
the weight of nights?

Gather round. We will now:
Auction the sun
Pawn the moon
Barter for the stars
Steal space
Sell time

"I choose one at a time."
"I choose linearity."
"I choose the echo of my choosing."
"I choose totality."

Death wears a silk face,
insisting, with the tentative
touch of the lobotomized,
that choosing
is academic –

Never mind.

        Touch
me again.

        I am
larger than life.

Yes sir. Scrambled brains,
jewels, sausages.

        I
only take your order.

The kitchen is your mystery.

        The last line,
the signature, the end

Kitchen Meditation

Given, for instance, a room.
The hour is daisies in green glass,
Black cat shaped in sleep.
Space rhythmic and shared. Mirrors loom
in each atomic structure. Times pass,
and yet faith hesitates to leap.

Words are numb with relationship.
Center of perception the trip.

Who has seen the time we've been,
has known how space has occupied itself
with things. I am preoccupied
with being here. There is
                      stillness
and black cat, crushed oval
of mute suspension, clearly
another edge. Of the world
expanding. Given a room.
Honor the tree soul of the wooden table,

Woman. Honor the fire. Emptiness
of word to being. For
                            it has all
been, and now
is geometric diagram or focus, analyzed,
beside the point,
chosen neither for meaning or form,
but for each unique despairing.

Suicide Notes

I

I have doubts.
About everything.
I doubt every choice
I have made.
I pray to be more loving, wiser.
I need to be stronger.
Here comes the inevitable.

Suicide Notes

II

Please, she begs of time, I have died
but
do not throw away all this paper
until someone
has read the words

flames, in THIS instant,
learn to read.

Suicide Notes

III

i am unfit to live
i have not learned
survival
i am dead

words are the ghost of me

Suicide Notes

IV

to be so naked
hard and dead
with a gun in your hand
with a gun in your hand
and your mouth that never grows old
your last breath warm as a june rose
between your teeth

how reciprocal
our deaths are become

Suicide Notes

V

between music and lyric
certain interval

measured relationship

i word; you song
we breathe
we beat our heart

we heartbeat

we process

between us
how much
potential
how much
nothing

we root in specific
image

i.e.
the mooncurve of our harp

Suicide Notes

VI

BLIND MAN SEEING MOON

She placed his fingers on the slender wood frame
of a small harp. This is how wood is, she told his feeling.
Then she placed a sword tip to his palm. Yet moon is also
this, she told his touching. But, she told him, and this he had
trouble learning to see, moon is very far away. You could hear
the moon's distance, if the moon were a music you could hear,
and the distance would be very far.

She told his blind ear of the phases of the moon, as it
appeared to change, revealing opposition.

She gave him as much of the moon as any one could,
and told him of children who cry for the moon.

All night long the essence of moon is sought.

Journey

As if with fingertips and tongue,
those keenest skins, those eyes
of touch; as if with probe
or grope or snaking journeys
against all stasis and of change; as if we could
know, at this once, what it is
we are given to feel.

The Dream of the Poet Superiors

In the first evening lamplight
My treasures lost their weight,
Lost their skin and lost their heat,
A ghost town's thin charade.
The cooking pots dissolved between
My hand's grasp and the flame
And my dear bed that rocked my head
Became a swimming swan.

At the first evening lamplight
All my treasures lost their name,
And I was dense and gummy
In my crackling paper house.
The evening held its breath,
A cornered frightened mouse,
At the first evening lamplight
In the whisper of a dream.

In the first evening starshine
I let two strangers in,
Took their hats and coats and shoes
and bid them welcome home.

Took their green and silver cloaks,
Led them through the hall,
Watched the flicker of firelight
Trace them to the wall.

And they were more elastic
Than I could bear to see,
Glowing like two candles
One each to a side of me –
Glowing like two candles
Thin and silky-pale,
From starshine to the morning blush
They sat and spun their tale.

The echo of the harp in the long long hall,
The song of the Poet Superiors.

The song they sang began with sound
And let no meaning by,
The second hour the song they spun
Took on a keening cry.
That second hour they spun a song
That splintered into word,
The more I tried to learn their tune
The more disdain I heard.

They sang to each and not to me
As if beneath some sea.
A storm roiled in the sodden sky
With grim finality.
And though they talked of poetry
And other graceful plays
All night I tossed upon the waves
Of storm and felt afraid.

The voices of the sea foam, the tang of salt upon my sheets,
A trickle of sand upon the morning floor.
Putting aside the purple robes of sleep,
We wake naked into yellow air –

There is no grace of memory
No hour of sweet recall:
The songs were sung, the harp was struck
And shadows gripped the wall.
The fire flickered high and then
The fire flickered low,
Out the door that in the door
They came to come no more.

It's not that I will search for them
For they are gone from me,
It's not that I will yearn for them
Or cling to memory,
But at the evening lamplight
My treasures lost their name
My paper house is ashes
And my soul is not the same.

Now everything I handle
Turns molten at my touch,
And everything I needed
I do not need so much,
For at the evening starshine
I open wide my door
In the struggle of the roaring wind
I hear a harp once more.

Sonnet—And If the Skies

And if the skies of night are but a glass
In which we see the darkness of shared soul
And if each fated moment come, then pass,
To teach eternity as something whole:
Within such mirror let us know our pain
Within such vision let us know our pleasure.
Reverse the picture: Abel lies yet slain,
Released to death. And when we take the measure
Of suffering, and joy, we see but dimly
That Cain's condemned to life and thus to sorrow.
Such mirrorings contain truth given grimly;
His brother's bliss is that he's no tomorrow.
The skies of dawn give promise of such light
That we forget the truth of skies at night.